meals in minutes

weeknight suppers

RECIPES
Melanie Barnard

PHOTOGRAPHS
Tucker + Hossler

weldon**owen**

contents

20 MINUTES START TO FINISH

about this book

Today, we care more than ever about the food we eat. Yet we also have less time to cook. Meals in Minutes *Weeknight Suppers* is specifically designed for busy people who want to put delicious, fresh food on the table—even on weeknights when life is at its most hectic. These carefully crafted recipes will help you create healthy, satisfying meals with surprisingly little effort.

Recipes such as a Thai-inspired Lime Shrimp with Coconut Rice, a rich Chicken Corn Chowder, and a remarkably simple Steak with Herb Butter are made with just a handful of well-chosen ingredients. Most recipes can be served as complete one-dish dinners, or can be rounded out with a simple accompaniment, such as roasted potatoes or a crisp green salad. With these recipes and the helpful tips in Meals in Minutes *Weeknight Suppers,* you'll find that dinner time can be a source of pleasure instead of stress.

20 minutes
start to finish

steaks with herb butter

Unsalted butter,
3 tablespoons, at room
temperature

Fresh chives, 2 tablespoons
snipped

Fresh rosemary,
1 tablespoon minced

**Salt and freshly ground
pepper**

Rib-eye steaks, 4, each
about 1 inch (2.5 cm) thick

SERVES 4

1 Prepare the herb butter
In a small dish, stir together the butter, chives, rosemary, and a pinch each of salt and pepper.

2 Cook the steaks
Meanwhile, prepare a gas or charcoal grill for direct-heat grilling over high heat and oil the grill rack. Or, preheat a broiler (grill). Season the steaks generously with salt and pepper, patting it firmly into the meat. Place the steaks on the grill rack, or put them on a baking sheet and place under the broiler. Cook, turning once, for 6–8 minutes total for medium-rare, or until done to your liking. Divide the steaks among 4 plates, top with the herb butter, and serve.

cook's tip

To complete the menu, serve the veal atop orzo pasta tossed with melted butter and a squeeze of lemon. Pass a side dish of braised spinach at the table.

veal cutlets
gremolata

1 Prepare the gremolata

Grate 1 tablespoon zest from the lemons and squeeze 2 tablespoons juice. Set the juice aside. In a small bowl, stir together the zest, parsley, and garlic. Set aside.

2 Cook the veal

Season the veal with salt and pepper. In a large frying pan over medium-high heat, melt 1½ tablespoons of the butter. Add half of the veal and cook, turning once, until browned, about 2 minutes total. Transfer to a plate. Repeat with 1½ tablespoons of the butter and the remaining veal.

3 Prepare the sauce

Melt the remaining 1 tablespoon butter in the same frying pan over medium-high heat. Add half of the *gremolata* and cook, stirring constantly, for 1 minute. Add the wine and stir, scraping up the browned bits on the pan bottom. Cook the sauce until reduced by half, about 2 minutes. Stir in the reserved lemon juice and season to taste with salt and pepper. Return the veal and any juices from the plate to the pan and simmer for 1–2 minutes to heat through. Sprinkle with the remaining *gremolata* and serve.

Lemons, 2

Fresh flat-leaf (Italian) parsley, ¼ cup (⅓ oz/10 g) minced

Garlic, 3 cloves, minced

Veal scallops, 8, about 1½ lb (750 g) total weight, pounded to about ¼-inch (6-mm) thickness

Salt and freshly ground pepper

Unsalted butter, 4 tablespoons (2 oz/60 g)

Dry white wine, ¾ cup (6 fl oz/180 ml)

SERVES 4

tandoori-style halibut

Plain yogurt, 1 cup
(8 oz/250 g)

Lemon juice, from ½ lemon

Ginger, 2 tablespoons grated

Yellow onion, 1 small, finely
chopped

Garlic, 2 cloves, minced

Ground cumin, 1 teaspoon

Ground turmeric,
1 teaspoon

Ground coriander,
½ teaspoon

Ground allspice,
½ teaspoon

Cayenne pepper,
¼ teaspoon

Salt

Halibut fillets, 4, about
1½ lb (750 g) total weight,
skin removed

Steamed white rice,
for serving

SERVES 4

1 **Prepare the yogurt marinade**
In a shallow glass or ceramic dish just large enough
to hold the halibut fillets in a single layer, stir together the yogurt,
lemon juice, ginger, onion, garlic, cumin, turmeric, coriander,
allspice, cayenne, and ½ teaspoon salt. Add the halibut to the
marinade and turn to coat.

2 **Cook the fish**
Meanwhile, prepare a gas or charcoal grill for direct-heat
grilling over medium-high heat and oil the grill rack. Or, preheat
a broiler (grill). When ready to cook, remove the halibut from
the marinade, discarding the marinade. Place on the grill rack,
or put on a baking sheet and place under the broiler. Cook,
turning once, until opaque throughout, 8–10 minutes. Spoon
the rice onto 4 plates, top with the halibut, and serve.

cook's tip

You can substitute 1 tablespoon *garam masala*—a classic Indian spice mixture—for the cumin, turmeric, coriander, allspice, and cayenne pepper. Look for *garam masala* in South Asian markets and well-stocked grocery stores.

miso-glazed salmon with bok choy

1 Marinate the fish

In a shallow glass or ceramic dish just large enough to hold the salmon fillets in a single layer, stir together the miso, mirin, sake, brown sugar, and soy sauce. Add the salmon to the marinade and turn to coat. Let stand at room temperature for 10 minutes, turning the fillets occasionally. Alternatively, cover and let marinate in the refrigerator for up to 2 days.

2 Cook the fish

Preheat the broiler (grill). Remove the fillets from the marinade, reserving the marinade. Place the fillets on a foil-lined rimmed baking sheet or broiler pan. Add the bok choy to the reserved marinade and turn to coat. Remove the bok choy, reserving the marinade, and arrange around the salmon. Place under the broiler and broil (grill) until the fillets and bok choy are caramelized and lightly charred on the edges, 3–4 minutes. Carefully turn the fillets and bok choy, and brush with the reserved marinade. Broil until the salmon is slightly charred on the outside and just cooked throughout and the bok choy is tender-crisp, 3–4 minutes longer. Divide the salmon and bok choy among 4 plates and serve.

White or yellow miso, 1/2 cup (5 oz/155 g)

Mirin or dry sherry, 1/3 cup (3 fl oz/80 ml)

Sake or dry white wine, 1/4 cup (2 fl oz/60 ml)

Light brown sugar, 3 tablespoons firmly packed

Soy sauce, 2 tablespoons

Salmon fillets, 4, about 1 1/2 lb (750 g) total weight, skin removed

Baby bok choy, 2 or 3 heads, cut in half lengthwise

SERVES 4

17

sausages with white beans

Hot or sweet Italian sausages, 8 small or 4 large, about 1½ lb (750 g) total weight

Dry white wine, 1 cup (8 fl oz/250 ml)

Olive oil, 2 tablespoons

Yellow onion, 1, finely chopped

Red bell pepper (capsicum), 1 large, seeded and chopped

Garlic, 2 cloves, minced

White beans such as cannellini or Great Northern, 2 cans (14 oz/ 440 g each), drained and rinsed

Fresh oregano, 2 tablespoons minced

Chicken broth, ¾ cup (6 fl oz/180 ml)

Salt and freshly ground pepper

Arugula (rocket), 2–3 cups (2–3 oz/60–90 g)

SERVES 4

1 Cook the sausages

Prick the sausages in a few places with a fork and place them in a large frying pan with a lid. Add ½ cup (4 fl oz/125 ml) of the wine. Bring to a boil over medium-high heat, cover, reduce the heat to medium-low, and simmer for 5 minutes. Uncover the pan, raise the heat to medium-high, and cook the sausages, turning occasionally, until well browned, 8–10 minutes. Transfer to a plate.

2 Cook the vegetables

While the sausages are cooking, in a separate large frying pan over medium-high heat, warm the oil. Add the onion and bell pepper and cook, stirring occasionally, until softened and beginning to brown, about 5 minutes. Add the garlic and cook, stirring constantly, for 30 seconds. Add the beans, oregano, the remaining ½ cup (4 fl oz/250 ml) wine, and the broth. Bring to a boil, reduce the heat to medium, and simmer, uncovered, until half of the liquid is evaporated, 4–5 minutes.

3 Finish the dish

Add the sausages to the pan with the beans and simmer for about 1 minute to warm through. Season to taste with salt and pepper. Divide the sausages, beans, and arugula among 4 plates, drizzle with any liquid in the pan, and serve.

cook's tip

You can substitute 2–3 cups
(2–3 oz/60–90 g) sliced
radicchio or chopped escarole
(Batavian endive) for the
arugula. Add it to the frying
pan with the onion and bell
pepper in step 2.

cook's tip

In its traditional form, Alsatian *choucroute garnie* calls for serving sauerkraut with a variety of fresh and cured meats. In this easy version, smoked pork chops and sausages top the sauerkraut. Round out the meal with a salad of sturdy greens with blue cheese, hearty pumpernickel bread, and boiled potatoes.

quick
choucroute

1 Cook the sausages

In a large frying pan over medium-high heat, warm the oil. Add the sausages, cut side down, and cook until browned, 3–4 minutes. Turn the sausages, add the onion, and cook, stirring occasionally, until the onion is softened, 4–5 minutes. Add the apple and cook, stirring occasionally, until the apple is softened and the onion is golden, about 3 minutes.

2 Simmer the sauerkraut and meat

Stir in the sauerkraut, bay leaf, caraway seeds, juniper berries, and wine. Add the pork chops in a single layer. Bring to a simmer over medium-high heat, reduce the heat to medium-low, cover, and cook for 10–12 minutes to blend the flavors. Remove and discard the bay leaf. Season to taste with pepper. Divide the choucroute among 4 plates and serve.

Olive oil, 3 tablespoons

Kielbasa, bratwurst, or knockwurst, or a combination, ¾ lb (375 g), cut in half lengthwise

Yellow onion, 1, sliced

Tart apple such as Granny Smith, 1, peeled, halved, cored, and sliced

Sauerkraut, 1 lb (500 g), well drained

Bay leaf, 1

Caraway seeds, 2 teaspoons

Juniper berries, 1 teaspoon, lightly crushed

Dry white wine, 1 cup (8 fl oz/250 ml)

Smoked pork chops, 4, each 4–6 oz (125–185 g)

Freshly ground pepper

SERVES 4

21

pork cutlets
with mustard sauce

Boneless center-cut pork loin chops, 4, each about 6 oz (185 g)

Salt and freshly ground pepper

Mustard seeds, 1 tablespoon

Unsalted butter, 3 tablespoons

Shallots, 2, minced

Dry white wine, ⅓ cup (3 fl oz/80 ml)

Chicken broth, ⅓ cup (3 fl oz/80 ml)

Heavy (double) cream, ⅓ cup (3 fl oz/80 ml)

Honey Dijon mustard, 2 tablespoons

SERVES 4

1 Cook the pork

Season the pork chops with salt, pepper, and the mustard seeds, patting them firmly into the meat. In a large frying pan over medium-high heat, melt the butter. Working in batches if necessary, add the pork chops and cook, turning once, until golden on the outside and barely pink in the center, about 8 minutes total. Transfer to a plate.

2 Make the sauce

Add the shallots to the drippings in the pan, reduce the heat to medium, and cook, stirring, for 1 minute. Add the wine and broth, stir, and cook, scraping up the browned bits on the pan bottom, for about 1 minute. Add the cream and mustard and cook, stirring, until smooth and bubbly, about 1 minute. Return the pork and any juices from the plate to the pan. Simmer until the pork is heated through, about 1 minute. Season to taste with salt and pepper. Divide the pork and sauce among 4 plates and serve.

cook's tip

To complete the menu, sauté
young, tender bitter greens such
as dandelion or collard greens
in butter. Drizzle with a few drops
of balsamic or sherry vinegar just
before serving.

cook's tip

You can also make satay with beef or shrimp (prawns). Substitute 1½ lb (750 g) beef chuck steak, cut into thick strips, or 24 medium shrimp, peeled and deveined. Add to the marinade and proceed as directed, adjusting the cooking time as needed.

thai
chicken satay

1 Marinate the chicken

Place 8 bamboo skewers in cold water to soak until ready to use. Grate 1 teaspoon zest from the limes and squeeze ¼ cup (2 fl oz/60 ml) juice. In a glass or ceramic bowl, whisk together the lime zest and juice, vinegar, and peanut butter until smooth. Stir in the cilantro, ginger, garlic, soy sauce, brown sugar, and sesame oil. Reserve about ½ cup (4 fl oz/120 ml) of the mixture in a separate bowl for use as a sauce. Add the chicken to the marinade and turn to coat. Let stand at room temperature for at least 10 minutes, or cover and refrigerate for up to 2 hours.

2 Cook the chicken

Meanwhile, prepare a gas or charcoal grill for direct-heat grilling over medium-high heat and oil the grill rack. Or, preheat a broiler (grill). When ready to cook, remove the chicken from the marinade, discarding the marinade. Divide the strips among the 8 skewers, threading the strips on lengthwise. Place the skewers on the grill rack, or put them on a baking sheet and place under the broiler. Cook, turning once, until seared on the outside and opaque throughout, about 6 minutes total. Divide the lettuce, cucumber slices, and chicken skewers among 4 plates. Drizzle with some of the reserved sauce and serve, passing additional sauce at the table.

Limes, 2 large

Rice vinegar, ½ cup
(4 fl oz/125 ml)

Chunky peanut butter,
⅓ cup (3½ oz/105 g)

**Fresh cilantro (fresh
coriander),** ¼ cup
(⅓ oz/10 g) minced

Ginger, 1 tablespoon minced

Garlic, 3 cloves, minced

Soy sauce, 3 tablespoons

Light brown sugar,
3 tablespoons firmly packed

Asian sesame oil,
1 tablespoon

**Skinless, boneless chicken
breast halves,** 4, about
1½ lb (750 g) total weight,
cut into thick strips

Romaine (cos) lettuce,
1 small head, cored and
leaves shredded

Cucumber, 1, peeled and
sliced

SERVES 4

lemongrass chicken & asparagus

Skinless, boneless chicken breast halves, 4, about 1½ lb (750 g) total weight, cut into thin strips

Salt and freshly ground pepper

Peanut or canola oil, 2 tablespoons (1 fl oz/30 ml)

Green (spring) onions, ¾ cup (2½ oz/75 g) thinly sliced

Ginger, 2 tablespoons minced

Lemongrass, 1 stalk, bulb part only, trimmed and finely chopped

Garlic, 3 cloves, minced

Slender asparagus, ½ lb (250 g), trimmed and sliced on the diagonal

Chicken broth, ¾ cup (6 fl oz/180 ml)

Asian fish sauce, 2 tablespoons

Peanuts, ¼ cup (1½ oz/45 g) chopped

Steamed white rice, for serving

SERVES 4

1 Stir-fry the chicken

Season the chicken lightly with salt and pepper. In a wok or frying pan over high heat, warm the oil. Add the chicken and stir-fry until golden on the outside and opaque throughout, 2–3 minutes. Transfer to a plate. Add the green onions and stir-fry until fragrant, 1–2 minutes. Add the ginger, lemongrass, and garlic and stir-fry for 30 seconds. Add the asparagus and stir-fry just until tender-crisp, 2–3 minutes.

2 Finish the dish

Add the broth and fish sauce to the pan and bring to a simmer. Return the chicken and any juices from the plate to the pan, reduce the heat to medium-low, and simmer for 1 minute to heat through. Sprinkle with the peanuts. Spoon the rice onto individual plates, top with the chicken and asparagus, and serve.

cook's tip

Lemongrass is available in many markets, but if you can't find it, substitute 1 tablespoon lemon juice and 2 teaspoons grated lemon zest. Add the juice and zest to the pan along with the garlic and ginger in step 1.

five-spice scallops with noodles

1 Prepare the oranges and noodles

Grate 1 teaspoon zest from the oranges and squeeze ½ cup (4 fl oz/125 ml) juice, and set both aside. Bring a large pot of water to a boil. Add the noodles to the boiling water and cook, stirring occasionally, until the noodles are tender, according to the package directions. Drain and set aside.

2 Cook the scallops

While the noodles are cooking, sprinkle the scallops on both sides with the five-spice powder and season lightly with salt and pepper. In a large frying pan over high heat, warm 3 tablespoons of the oil. Working in batches if necessary, add the scallops in a single layer to the pan and cook until well browned on the bottom, about 1 minute. Turn the scallops and cook until well browned on the outside and just opaque in the center, 1–2 minutes. Transfer the scallops to a plate.

3 Cook the vegetables

Add the remaining 1 tablespoon oil to the same frying pan over high heat. Add the ginger and garlic and stir-fry just until fragrant, about 30 seconds. Add the sugar snap peas and stir-fry just until tender-crisp, about 1 minute. Stir in the orange zest and juice, wine, and soy sauce and cook until slightly reduced, 1–2 minutes. Add the cooked noodles and green onions and toss gently to combine. Divide the noodles and snap peas among 4 plates, top with the scallops, and serve.

Oranges, 2

Salt and freshly ground pepper

Fresh Chinese egg noodles, ½ lb (250 g)

Large sea scallops, 1¼ lb (625 g) total weight

Chinese five-spice powder, 2 teaspoons

Peanut or canola oil, 4 tablespoons (2 fl oz/60 ml)

Ginger, 1 tablespoon finely chopped

Garlic, 3 cloves, minced

Sugar snap peas, 1¼ lb (625 g)

Dry white wine, ½ cup (4 fl oz/125 ml)

Soy sauce, 2 tablespoons

Green (spring) onions, 4, white and pale green parts, chopped

SERVES 4

chimichurri
steak

Olive oil, ⅓ cup
(3 fl oz/80 ml)

Sherry vinegar, ⅓ cup
(3 fl oz/80 ml)

Fresh oregano leaves,
3 tablespoons

**Fresh flat-leaf (Italian)
parsley,** ½ cup (½ oz/15 g)
coarsely chopped

Garlic, 7 cloves, coarsely
chopped

Red pepper flakes,
½–¾ teaspoon

T-bone steaks, 4, each
about 1 inch (2.5 cm) thick

Salt

SERVES 4

1 Marinate the steaks

In a food processor, combine the oil, vinegar, oregano, parsley, and garlic, and process until finely chopped. Pour into a shallow glass or ceramic dish large enough to hold the steaks in a single layer, and stir in the red pepper flakes to taste. Season the steaks with salt, then add them to the marinade and turn to coat. Let stand at room temperature for 10 minutes.

2 Cook the steaks

Meanwhile, prepare a gas or charcoal grill for direct-heat grilling over high heat and oil the grill rack. Or, preheat a broiler (grill). When ready to cook, remove the steaks from the marinade, reserving the marinade. Place the steaks on the grill rack, or put them on a baking sheet and place under the broiler. Brush the steaks with the remaining marinade. Cook, carefully turning once, for about 8 minutes total for medium-rare, or until done to your liking. Divide the steaks among 4 plates and serve.

cook's tip

Roasted rosemary potato wedges are an excellent accompaniment to these flavorful steaks. Toss Yukon gold potato wedges with a little olive oil, 1 tablespoon minced rosemary, and salt. Roast in a 375°F (190°C) oven until tender, about 30 minutes.

cook's tip

This recipe can be completed with a simple side dish of herbed white beans. Drain and rinse 1–2 cans (14 oz/440 g each) of cannellini beans. Briefly sauté the beans in a few tablespoons of olive oil with minced garlic, then toss with a drizzle of champagne vinegar and 1 tablespoon chopped fresh marjoram. Season to taste with salt and pepper.

lamb chops with garlic & rosemary

1 Marinate the lamb

Grate 2 teaspoons zest from the lemons and squeeze ½ cup (4 fl oz/125 ml) juice. In a shallow glass or ceramic dish just large enough to hold the lamb in a single layer, combine the oil and anchovies, if using, and mash with a spoon to form a paste. Stir in the lemon zest and juice, rosemary, and garlic. Season the lamb with pepper. Place in the marinade and turn to coat. Let stand at room temperature for 10 minutes, or cover and refrigerate for up to overnight.

2 Cook the lamb

Meanwhile, prepare a gas or charcoal grill for direct-heat grilling over high heat and oil the grill rack. Or, preheat a broiler (grill). When ready to cook, remove the lamb from the marinade, discarding the marinade. Place the chops on the grill rack, or put them on a baking sheet and place under the broiler. Cook, turning once, for about 10 minutes total for medium-rare, or until done to your liking. Divide the chops among 4 plates and serve.

Lemons, 3

Olive oil, ¼ cup (2 fl oz/60 ml)

Anchovies, 5 fillets (optional)

Fresh rosemary, 1 tablespoon minced

Garlic, 4 cloves, minced

Lamb loin chops, 8, each about 6 oz (185 g) and 1 inch (2.5 cm) thick

Freshly ground pepper

SERVES 4

30 minutes
start to finish

farfalle with salsa cruda

Tomatoes, 1 ½ lb (750 g), cored and coarsely chopped

Garlic, 2 cloves, minced

Fresh basil, ½ cup (¾ oz/20 g) slivered

Olive oil, ½ cup (4 fl oz/125 ml)

Balsamic vinegar, 3 tablespoons

Red pepper flakes, ½ teaspoon

Smoked or regular mozzarella cheese, ½ lb (250 g), cubed

Pine nuts, ¼ cup (1 ¼ oz/36 g)

Salt and freshly ground black pepper

Farfalle, penne, or other medium-sized pasta, 1 lb (500 g)

Prosciutto, 2 oz (60 g), thinly sliced and chopped

SERVES 4

1 Prepare the sauce
In a large bowl, combine the tomatoes, garlic, basil, oil, vinegar, and red pepper flakes. Stir well and let stand at room temperature for about 15 minutes to blend the flavors. Stir in the mozzarella and let stand for about 10 minutes longer.

2 Toast the pine nuts
Meanwhile, in a small, dry frying pan over medium-high heat, toast the pine nuts, stirring often, until fragrant and pale gold, 1–2 minutes. Transfer to a plate and set aside.

3 Cook the pasta
At the same time, bring a large pot of water to a boil. Add 2 tablespoons salt and the pasta and cook, stirring occasionally, until al dente, according to the package directions. Drain well and add the pasta to the sauce, along with the prosciutto and pine nuts. Toss to combine and slightly soften the cheese. Season to taste with salt and black pepper. Serve the pasta warm or at room temperature.

cook's tip

Make this dish in the summer when ripe, juicy tomatoes are abundant and you can choose from among many varieties, including heirlooms. At other times of the year, use meaty plum (Roma) tomatoes.

cook's tip

Because this simple variation
on chicken-noodle soup includes
so few ingredients, it is important
to use the best chicken broth or
stock you can find. Look for high-
quality broth in the freezer section
of gourmet groceries and well-
stocked supermarkets.

chicken & orzo soup

1 Sauté the vegetables

In a large saucepan over medium heat, melt the butter. Add the onion and sauté until translucent, 3–4 minutes. Add the carrots, celery, and marjoram and sauté until the vegetables are softened, about 3 minutes longer. Add the broth, raise the heat to medium-high, and simmer for 5 minutes to blend the flavors.

2 Cook the pasta

Add the pasta to the simmering soup and cook for 3–4 minutes until the pasta is al dente, according to the package directions. Add the spinach and the chicken and cook, stirring, until the spinach has wilted and the chicken is warmed through, about 1 minute. Season to taste with salt and pepper. Ladle the soup into individual bowls, sprinkle with some of the cheese, and serve. Pass the remaining cheese at the table.

Unsalted butter, 1 tablespoon

Yellow onion, 1 small, finely chopped

Carrots, 2, thinly sliced

Celery, 1 stalk, thinly sliced

Fresh marjoram, 2 tablespoons minced

Chicken broth, 8 cups (64 fl oz/2 l)

Orzo, pastina, or other small pasta shape, 3/4 cup (5 oz/155 g)

Baby spinach, 6 oz (185 g)

Cooked chicken, 3 cups (18 oz/560 g) shredded, homemade (page 76) or purchased

Salt and freshly ground pepper

Parmesan cheese, 1/2 cup (2 oz/60 g) freshly grated

SERVES 4

cuban
beef picadillo

Olive oil, 1 tablespoon

Yellow onion, 1, chopped

Lean ground (minced) beef chuck, 1 ½ lb (750 g) total weight

Garlic, 2 cloves, finely chopped

Chili powder, 2 tablespoons

Ground cinnamon, ¾ teaspoon

Ground allspice, ½ teaspoon

Diced tomatoes, 1 can (28 oz/875 g), with juice

Beef broth, 1¾ cups (14 fl oz/430 ml)

Raisins or currants, ⅔ cup (4 oz/125 g)

Tomato paste, 2 tablespoons

Red wine vinegar, ¼ cup (2 fl oz/60 ml)

Salt and freshly ground pepper

Steamed white rice, for serving

SERVES 4

1 Cook the meat and onion

In a large, deep frying pan over medium-high heat, warm the oil. Add the onion and sauté until translucent, 3–4 minutes. Add the beef and cook, stirring to break up any clumps, until the meat begins to brown, 7–8 minutes. Spoon off and discard the excess fat.

2 Cook the tomatoes and seasonings

Stir in the garlic, chili powder, cinnamon, and allspice and cook, stirring frequently, for 1 minute. Stir in the tomatoes with their juice, broth, raisins, tomato paste, and vinegar. Bring to a simmer, reduce the heat to medium, and cook, uncovered, until thickened to a stewlike consistency, 10–15 minutes. Season to taste with salt and pepper. Divide the steamed rice among 4 shallow bowls, ladle the *picadillo* on top, and serve.

cook's tip

This Cuban-inspired dish is also
delicious wrapped in corn tortillas
as a filling for soft tacos or in
flour tortillas for burritos. Or, serve
it over spaghetti and top with
shredded cheddar cheese for
a quick version of Cincinnati chili.

chicken & corn
chowder

1 Cook the bacon

In a saucepan over medium heat, fry the bacon until crisp, about 5 minutes. Using a slotted spoon, transfer to paper towels to drain. Pour off all but 3 tablespoons of the drippings.

2 Cook the vegetables and chicken

Add the bell pepper, corn, and potatoes to the same pan over medium heat. Cook, stirring frequently, until the peppers are just softened and the corn and potatoes are lightly tinged with gold, 4–5 minutes. Add the broth and wine, bring to a boil, cover, and cook until the potatoes are almost tender, about 5 minutes. Add the chicken and cook, covered, until opaque throughout, 5–7 minutes.

3 Finish the chowder

Stir in the green onions, thyme, and half-and-half. Bring to a simmer over medium heat, reduce the heat to medium-low, and cook, uncovered, until heated through, about 3 minutes. Season to taste with salt and pepper. Ladle the chowder into bowls, sprinkle with the bacon, and serve.

Bacon, 4 slices, chopped

Red bell pepper (capsicum), 1 large, seeded and chopped

Fresh or frozen corn kernels, 4 cups (1½ lb/ 750 g)

Yukon gold potatoes, ¾ lb (375 g), cut into ½-inch (12-mm) chunks

Chicken broth, 3 cups (24 fl oz/750 ml)

Dry white wine, ½ cup (4 fl oz/125 ml)

Skinless, boneless chicken thighs, ¾ lb (375 g) total weight, cut into ½-inch (12-mm) chunks

Green (spring) onions, 6, white and pale green parts, thinly sliced

Fresh thyme, 3 tablespoons minced

Half-and-half (half cream), 2½ cups (20 fl oz/625 ml)

Salt and freshly ground pepper

SERVES 4

thai
chicken curry

Limes, 2

Skinless, boneless chicken breast halves, 4, about 1 ½ lb (750 g) total weight

Salt and freshly ground pepper

Peanut or canola oil, 3 tablespoons

Green beans, ¼ lb (125 g), trimmed and cut into 2-inch (5-cm) lengths

Thai red curry paste, 1 ½ tablespoons

Unsweetened coconut milk, 1 cup (8 fl oz/250 ml)

Chicken broth, ⅔ cup (5 fl oz/160 ml)

Asian fish sauce, 1 tablespoon

Green (spring) onions, 6, including white and tender green parts, sliced

Fresh basil, preferably Thai, ¼ cup (⅓ oz/10 g) slivered

Steamed white rice, for serving

SERVES 4

1 Cook the chicken and green beans

Grate 1 teaspoon zest from the limes and squeeze ¼ cup (2 fl oz/60 ml) juice. Set aside. Cut the chicken into thin strips and season with salt and pepper. In a large frying pan or wok over medium-high heat, warm the oil. Add the chicken and cook, turning occasionally, until golden, 4–5 minutes. Using a slotted spoon, transfer to a plate. Add the green beans and cook, stirring frequently, just until tender-crisp, 2–3 minutes. Transfer to the plate with the chicken.

2 Prepare the sauce

Stir the curry paste into the pan over medium-high heat. Stir in the coconut milk, broth, and fish sauce. Bring to a simmer and stir, scraping up the browned bits on the pan bottom. Stir in the reserved lime zest and juice.

3 Finish the curry

Return the chicken and green beans to the pan and stir to combine with the sauce. Simmer until the chicken is opaque throughout, 3–4 minutes. Stir in the green onions and basil. Spoon the rice into bowls, top with the curry, and serve.

cook's tip

Thai basil, with its purple buds, pointed, bright green leaves, and purple stems, has a lemony flavor that adds a distinctive taste to this curry and other Southeast Asian dishes. It can be found in most Asian markets and many well-stocked supermarkets.

cook's tip

If you can't find escarole, you can use 1 bunch Swiss chard, stems removed and leaves shredded.

ham, bean & escarole soup

1 Cook the ham
In a large saucepan over medium-high heat, warm 2 tablespoons of the oil. Add the ham and sauté until golden and crisp, about 3 minutes. Using a slotted spoon, transfer to a plate and set aside. Reduce the heat to medium and add more oil if necessary. Add the onion and sauté until softened, about 4 minutes. Add the garlic and sauté for 30 seconds.

2 Cook the escarole and beans
Add the broth to the saucepan and bring to a boil over medium-high heat. Add the escarole and cook, stirring, until wilted, 2–3 minutes. Add the beans, rosemary, and red pepper flakes. Bring to a boil, reduce the heat to medium-low, and simmer for 5 minutes to heat through.

3 Finish the soup
Add the ham to the pan and cook, stirring occasionally, until heated through, 2–3 minutes. Using the back of a large spoon, mash some of the beans to thicken the soup slightly. Simmer for 2 minutes longer. Ladle the soup into bowls, sprinkle with some of the cheese, and serve. Pass the remaining cheese at the table.

Olive oil, 2–3 tablespoons

Ham, ½ lb (250 g), thickly sliced and cut into cubes

Yellow onion, 1, finely chopped

Garlic, 4 cloves, minced

Chicken broth, 7 cups (56 fl oz/1.75 l)

Escarole (Batavian endive), 1 head, cored, leaves torn into pieces

White beans such as cannellini or Great Northern, 2 cans (14 oz/ 440 g each), drained and rinsed

Fresh rosemary, 2 tablespoons minced

Red pepper flakes, ¼ teaspoon

Parmesan cheese, ½ cup (2 oz/60 g) freshly grated

SERVES 4

47

polenta with vegetable ragout

Olive oil, 4 tablespoons
(2 fl oz/60 ml)

Yellow onion, 1, chopped

Garlic, 3 cloves, finely
chopped

Zucchini (courgette),
1, sliced

**Mixed wild and cultivated
fresh mushrooms,** ¾ lb
(375 g), trimmed and sliced

Plum (Roma) tomatoes,
½ lb (250 g), seeded and
chopped

Fresh rosemary,
1 tablespoon minced

**Marsala, sherry, or other
fortified wine,** ¼ cup
(2 fl oz/60 ml)

**Salt and freshly ground
pepper**

**Vegetable or chicken
broth,** 4 cups (32 fl oz/1 l)

Quick-cooking polenta,
1 cup (7 oz/220 g)

Parmesan cheese, ¼ cup
(1 oz/30 g) freshly grated

SERVES 4

1 Cook the vegetable ragout
In a large frying pan over medium heat, warm
3 tablespoons of the oil. Add the onion and sauté until softened,
about 4 minutes. Add the garlic, zucchini, and mushrooms and
cook, stirring occasionally, until the vegetables are softened,
4–5 minutes. Add the tomatoes, rosemary, Marsala, and about
½ teaspoon each salt and pepper. Continue to cook, stirring
frequently, until the tomatoes release their juices and are
softened, 3–4 minutes.

2 Prepare the polenta
Meanwhile, in a saucepan over high heat, bring the broth
to a boil. Whisk in the polenta and 1 teaspoon salt. Reduce the
heat to low and cook, stirring frequently, until the polenta is thick
and creamy, about 5 minutes. Remove from the heat and stir
in the remaining 1 tablespoon oil and the cheese. Spoon the
polenta into shallow bowls, top with the ragout, and serve.

cook's tip

Quick-cooking polenta is
available in most well-stocked
markets. If you can't find it,
use regular polenta and cook
it for 25–30 minutes, or use
cornmeal and cook it for
15–20 minutes.

cook's tip

Serve the chicken with grilled
sweet potato or yam wedges.
Toss the wedges with olive oil,
salt, and pepper and grill over
indirect heat until tender, about
30 minutes.

grilled mojo chicken

1 Marinate the chicken

Grate 2 teaspoons zest from the orange and squeeze 1/3 cup (3 fl oz/80 ml) juice. Grate 1 teaspoon zest from the limes and squeeze 1/4 cup (2 fl oz/60 ml) juice. In a shallow glass or ceramic dish just large enough to hold the chicken in a single layer, stir together the orange and lime zests and juices, 2 tablespoons of the parsley, the oregano, thyme, garlic, and cumin. Stir in the oil. Season the chicken generously with salt and pepper. Add the chicken to the marinade and turn to coat. Let stand at room temperature for 10 minutes, or cover and refrigerate for up to 2 hours.

2 Cook the chicken

Meanwhile, prepare a gas or charcoal grill for direct-heat grilling over medium-high heat and oil the grill rack. Or, preheat a broiler (grill). When ready to cook, remove the chicken from the marinade, discarding the marinade. Place on the grill rack, or put on a baking sheet and place under the broiler. Cook, turning once, until opaque throughout, 10–14 minutes. Divide the chicken among 4 plates, sprinkle with the remaining 2 tablespoons parsley, and serve.

Orange, 1

Limes, 2

Fresh flat-leaf (Italian) parsley, 4 tablespoons (1/3 oz/10 g) minced

Fresh oregano, 1 tablespoon minced

Fresh thyme, 1 tablespoon minced

Garlic, 3 cloves, minced

Ground cumin, 2 teaspoons

Olive oil, 1/4 cup (2 fl oz/60 ml)

Skinless, boneless chicken thighs or breast halves, 4, about 1 1/2 lb (750 g) total weight

Salt and freshly ground pepper

SERVES 4

51

moroccan lamb burgers

Lean ground (minced) lamb, 1 ½ lb (750 g) total weight

Fresh mint, 5 tablespoons (½ oz/15 g) minced

Fresh parsley, 5 tablespoons (½ oz/15 g) minced

Yellow onion, 1 small, finely chopped

Ground cumin, 1 ¼ teaspoons

Ground cinnamon, ½ teaspoon

Salt

Cayenne pepper, to taste

Plain yogurt, ½ cup (4 oz/125 g)

Plum (Roma) tomatoes, ¾ cup (4½ oz/140 g) diced

Pita breads, 4, cut into wedges

Cucumber, 1 large, halved lengthwise and thinly sliced crosswise

SERVES 4

1 **Prepare the lamb patties**
Prepare a charcoal or gas grill for direct-heat grilling over high heat. In a large bowl, using your hands, mix together the lamb, 4 tablespoons each of the mint and parsley, the onion, 1 teaspoon of the cumin, the cinnamon, ½ teaspoon salt, and a pinch of cayenne. Form the lamb mixture into 4 oval patties.

2 **Prepare the yogurt sauce**
In a small bowl, stir together the yogurt, the remaining mint and parsley, and the remaining cumin. Season to taste with salt and cayenne pepper. Set aside.

3 **Cook the lamb patties**
Oil the grill rack. Grill the lamb patties, turning once, for about 10 minutes total for medium, or until done to your liking. (Alternatively, cook the lamb patties on the stove top in a heavy frying pan over medium-high heat, turning once, for about 10 minutes total for medium.) Place a lamb patty on each of 4 plates, then top each patty with a spoonful of the yogurt sauce, sprinkle with the tomatoes, and serve along with the cucumber slices. Pass the remaining yogurt sauce and the pita breads at the table.

cook's tip

To make this into a complete
meal, serve the turkey cutlets
and gravy with creamy mashed
potatoes and sautéed green
beans. Reminiscent of an easy
Thanksgiving dinner, it's hearty
comfort food at its best.

turkey cutlets with herbed pan gravy

1 Cook the turkey

Season the turkey cutlets generously on both sides with salt and pepper. In a small bowl, combine half each of the sage, thyme, and marjoram. Sprinkle the herb mixture on the turkey, then pat it firmly into the meat. In a large frying pan over medium-high heat, melt 2 tablespoons of the butter. Add the turkey in a single layer and cook, turning once, until golden on the outside and opaque throughout, 6–8 minutes total. Transfer to a plate.

2 Make the gravy

Add the remaining 3 tablespoons butter to the pan and reduce the heat to medium. When the butter is melted, add the celery and onion and sauté until softened, about 5 minutes. Stir in the flour and cook, stirring constantly, until the mixture is thickened and begins to turn pale gold, 1–2 minutes. Slowly stir in the broth, Madeira, and the remaining sage, thyme, and marjoram. Cook, stirring constantly, until the gravy is smooth, thickened, and bubbly, 3–4 minutes.

3 Finish the dish

Return the turkey and any juices from the plate to the pan and simmer until heated through, about 1 minute. Divide the turkey and gravy among 4 plates and serve.

Turkey cutlets, 4, each about 6 oz (185 g) and ½ inch (12 mm) thick

Salt and freshly ground pepper

Fresh sage, 1 tablespoon minced

Fresh thyme, 1 tablespoon minced

Fresh marjoram, 1 tablespoon minced

Unsalted butter, 5 tablespoons (2½ oz/75 g)

Celery, 2 stalks, finely chopped

Yellow onion, 1 small, finely chopped

Flour, 3 tablespoons

Chicken broth, 2½ cups (20 fl oz/625 ml)

Madeira or sherry, 2 tablespoons

SERVES 4

lime shrimp with coconut rice

Unsalted butter,
5 tablespoons (2½ oz/75 g)

Long-grain white rice,
1 cup (7 oz/220 g)

Unsweetened coconut milk, 1¼ cups (10 fl oz/ 310 ml)

Lime, 1

Garlic, 6 cloves, minced

Large shrimp (prawns),
1 lb (500 g) total weight, peeled and deveined

Green (spring) onions,
8, white and pale green parts, thinly sliced

Fresh cilantro (fresh coriander), ¼ cup (⅓ oz/10 g) minced

SERVES 4

1 Cook the rice
In a saucepan over medium heat, melt 1 tablespoon of the butter. Add the rice and cook, stirring constantly, until the grains are well coated with the butter, about 1 minute. Stir in 1¼ cups (10 fl oz/310 ml) water and the coconut milk. Bring to a boil, reduce the heat to low, cover, and cook until the liquid is absorbed and the rice is tender, about 20 minutes.

2 Cook the shrimp
While the rice cooks, grate 1 teaspoon zest and squeeze 2 tablespoons juice from the lime. About 5 minutes before the rice is ready, in a large frying pan over medium heat, melt the remaining 4 tablespoons (2 oz/60 g) butter. Add the garlic and lime zest and juice and stir until the mixture is bubbly. Add the shrimp and green onions and sauté until the shrimp are just opaque throughout, about 3 minutes. Stir in about half of the cilantro.

3 Finish the rice
Fluff the rice and gently stir in the remaining cilantro. Divide the rice among 4 plates, top with the shrimp, and serve.

cook's tip

Some stores and fish markets
carry peeled and deveined shrimp,
which will save you quite a bit
of time. Avoid shrimp with
an "off" odor, a dull appearance,
or a gritty feel.

cook's tip

Frittatas usually include chopped vegetables and/or meat and highly seasoned cheeses, which makes them a great way to use up leftovers you have on hand.

herbed spinach frittata with feta

1 Cook the vegetables

In a heavy 10-inch (25-cm) ovenproof frying pan over medium heat, warm the oil. Add the onion and sauté just until softened, 3–4 minutes. Add the garlic, spinach, and roasted pepper and cook, stirring, until the spinach wilts, 1–2 minutes.

2 Prepare the frittata

While the vegetables are cooking, in a bowl, whisk together the eggs, oregano, mint, and ½ teaspoon each salt and pepper. Spread the vegetables evenly in the pan, then pour in the egg mixture. Reduce the heat to medium-low and cook, without stirring, until the edges begin to look set, about 3 minutes. Using a spatula, carefully lift up the edges of the frittata and let the uncooked egg run underneath. Continue to cook, without stirring, until the eggs are almost set on top, 5–8 minutes longer.

3 Finish the frittata

While the frittata is cooking, preheat the broiler (grill). Sprinkle the frittata with the feta cheese. Place the frittata under the broiler. Broil (grill) until the top is set and the cheese melts and is tinged with gold, about 3 minutes. Cut into wedges and serve directly from the pan.

Olive oil, 3 tablespoons

Red onion, 1 small, finely chopped

Garlic, 2 cloves, minced

Baby spinach, 6 oz (185 g)

Roasted red bell pepper (capsicum), ½ cup (2½ oz/75 g) chopped

Eggs, 8

Fresh oregano, 1 tablespoon minced

Fresh mint, 1 tablespoon minced

Salt and freshly ground pepper

Feta cheese, 1 cup (5 oz/155 g) crumbled

SERVES 4

59

balsamic chicken & peppers

Skinless, boneless chicken breast halves or thighs, 4, about 1½ lb (750 g) total weight

Salt and freshly ground pepper

Olive oil, 4 tablespoons (2 fl oz/60 ml)

Red bell pepper (capsicum), 1, seeded and sliced

Yellow bell pepper (capsicum), 1, seeded and sliced

Yellow onion, 1 large, thinly sliced

Garlic, 3 cloves, minced

Balsamic vinegar, 3 tablespoons

Fresh basil, ¼ cup (⅓ oz/10 g) minced

Fresh thyme, 1 tablespoon minced

SERVES 4

1 Cook the chicken
Season the chicken generously with salt and pepper. In a large frying pan over medium-high heat, warm 2 tablespoons of the oil. Add the chicken and cook, turning once, until golden brown, about 7 minutes total. Transfer to a plate.

2 Cook the vegetables
Add the remaining 2 tablespoons oil to the same pan over medium-high heat. Add the bell peppers and onion and sauté until softened, about 6 minutes. Add the garlic and sauté for 1 minute.

3 Finish the chicken
Add the vinegar and half each of the basil and thyme and stir, scraping up the browned bits on the pan bottom. Return the chicken and any juices from the plate to the pan, spooning the peppers over the chicken. Reduce the heat to medium and simmer until the chicken is opaque throughout, 2–3 minutes. Stir in the remaining basil and thyme and season to taste with salt and pepper. Divide among 4 plates and serve.

cook's tip

Roasted potato wedges go well
with this dish. Cut russet potatoes
into wedges and toss with olive
oil, salt, and pepper. Roast in a
375°F (190°C) oven until tender,
about 30 minutes.

cook's tip

Serve the kebabs over rice pilaf
or steamed long-grain white rice.
Accompany with thickly sliced
tomatoes drizzled with olive oil
and sprinkled with crumbled
feta cheese.

greek
lamb kebabs

1 Marinate the lamb

Place 8 bamboo skewers in cold water to soak until ready to use. Grate 3 teaspoons zest from the lemons and squeeze 5 tablespoons (2½ fl oz/75 ml) juice. In a shallow glass or ceramic dish just large enough to hold the lamb in a single layer, combine 2 teaspoons of the lemon zest, 3 tablespoons of the lemon juice, the oregano, half each of the green onions and garlic, and the oil. Season the lamb generously with salt and pepper. Add the lamb to the marinade and turn to coat. Let stand for 15 minutes at room temperature.

2 Make the yogurt sauce

While the lamb is marinating, in a small bowl, stir together the yogurt, cucumber, the remaining 1 teaspoon lemon zest and 2 tablespoons juice, and the remaining green onion and garlic. Season with salt and pepper. Cover and refrigerate for 15 minutes.

3 Cook the lamb

Prepare a gas or charcoal grill for direct-heat grilling over high heat and oil the grill rack. Or, preheat a broiler (grill). When ready to cook, remove the lamb from the marinade, discarding the marinade. Thread the lamb onto the skewers. Place on the grill rack, or put on a baking sheet and place under the broiler. Cook, turning once, for 6–7 minutes for medium-rare, or until done to your liking. Divide the skewers among 4 plates and serve with the yogurt sauce.

Lemons, 2 large

Fresh oregano,
2 tablespoons minced

Green (spring) onions,
5, white and pale green parts,
thinly sliced

Garlic, 5 cloves, minced

Olive oil, ¼ cup
(2 fl oz/60 ml)

Boneless lamb from leg,
1½ lb (750 g) total weight,
cut into 2-inch (5-cm) cubes

**Salt and freshly ground
pepper**

Plain yogurt, 1 cup
(8 oz/250 g)

Cucumber, 1 small, peeled,
seeded, and chopped

SERVES 4

63

spring vegetable risotto

Vegetable or chicken broth, 5 cups (40 fl oz/1.25 l)

Dry white wine, 1 1/2 cups (12 fl oz/375 ml)

Unsalted butter, 1 tablespoon

Olive oil, 3 tablespoons

Yellow onion, 1 small, finely chopped

Arborio rice, 2 cups (14 oz/440 g)

Zucchini (courgettes), 1 lb (500 g), cut into 1/2-inch (12-mm) chunks

Frozen baby peas, 2 cups (10 oz/315 g)

Fresh mint, 1/4 cup (1/3 oz/10 g) minced

Parmesan cheese, 2/3 cup (2 1/2 oz/75 g) freshly grated

Salt and freshly ground pepper

SERVES 4

1 Cook the risotto

In a saucepan over medium heat, bring the broth and wine to a gentle simmer, then maintain the simmer over low heat. Meanwhile, in a heavy-bottomed saucepan or Dutch oven over medium heat, melt the butter with 1 tablespoon of the oil. Add the onion and sauté until softened, about 4 minutes. Add the rice and cook, stirring constantly, until all the grains are opaque and well coated with the fat, about 1 minute. Add 2 cups (16 fl oz/500 ml) of the simmering broth mixture and cook, stirring frequently, until the liquid is absorbed, 3–4 minutes. Reduce the heat to medium-low and continue to add the liquid about 1 cup at a time, stirring occasionally, and adding more only after the previous addition has been absorbed.

2 Sauté the vegetables

While the rice is cooking, in a frying pan over medium heat, warm the remaining 2 tablespoons oil. Add the zucchini and sauté just until softened, about 4 minutes. Add the peas and cook, stirring, until thawed and heated through, about 2 minutes. Remove from the heat.

3 Finish the risotto

When the rice is tender and creamy but the grains are still al dente at the center, after about 22 minutes, stir in the sautéed vegetables and the mint and cook for 1 minute to heat through. Stir in the cheese. Season to taste with salt and pepper, divide among shallow bowls, and serve.

cook's tip

Many cooks are reluctant to make risotto at home because they believe it needs constant stirring. But in reality, the cook can be a bit more relaxed. As long as you pay attention to the amount of liquid and stir every few minutes, the results will be just as good.

thai beef
noodle salad

1 Marinate the steak and cook the noodles

In a shallow glass or ceramic dish just large enough to hold the steak, stir together the garlic, fish sauce, soy sauce, sugar, and ¼ cup (2 fl oz/60 ml) of the peanut oil. Pour ¼ cup of the marinade into a small bowl, cover, and refrigerate to use later as a vinaigrette. Season the steak with pepper. Add the steak to the marinade and turn to coat. Let stand at room temperature for 15 minutes. Meanwhile, bring a large pot of water to a boil. Add the vermicelli noodles and cook according to the package directions. Drain and set aside.

2 Cook the steak

While the steak is marinating, prepare a gas or charcoal grill for direct-heat grilling over high heat and oil the grill rack. Or, preheat a broiler (grill). When ready to cook, remove the beef from the marinade, discarding the marinade. Place on the grill rack, or put on a baking sheet and place under the broiler. Cook, turning once, for 10–12 minutes total for medium-rare, or until done to your liking. Transfer to a carving board and let rest for 5 minutes.

3 Make the vinaigrette and assemble the salad

Whisk the remaining ¼ cup oil and the vinegar into the reserved marinade. Season to taste with pepper. Cut the steak across the grain into thin slices. In a large bowl, combine the salad greens, vermicelli noodles, onion, basil, and steak slices. Drizzle with the vinaigrette and toss to combine. Divide among 4 plates and serve.

Garlic, 4 cloves, minced

Asian fish sauce, ¼ cup (2 fl oz/60 ml)

Soy sauce, 1½ tablespoons

Sugar, 2 teaspoons

Peanut oil, ½ cup (4 fl oz/120 ml)

Flank steak, 1½ lb (750 g)

Freshly ground pepper

Rice vermicelli noodles, ½ lb (250 g)

Rice vinegar, 2 tablespoons

Mixed salad greens, 6 cups (6 oz/185 g)

Red onion, 1 small, halved and thinly sliced

Fresh basil, preferably Thai, ½ cup (½ oz/15 g)

SERVES 4

italian
seafood stew

Olive oil, 3 tablespoons

Leek, 1, including pale green parts, halved, washed, and thinly sliced

Fennel bulb, 1 small, trimmed and chopped

Garlic, 3 cloves, minced

Diced tomatoes, 1 can (14½ oz/455 g), with juice

Fish stock, 1½ cups (12 fl oz/375 ml)

Dry red or white wine, 1 cup (8 fl oz/250 ml)

Fresh thyme, 1 tablespoon chopped

Salt and freshly ground pepper

Firm white fish fillets such as halibut, ¾ lb (375 g) total weight, cut into 1-inch (2.5-cm) chunks

Small mussels or clams, 18, well scrubbed

Fresh lump crabmeat, 6 oz (185 g), picked over for shell fragments

SERVES 4

1 Cook the vegetables
In a large saucepan or Dutch oven over medium heat, warm the oil. Add the leek and fennel and sauté until softened, about 5 minutes. Stir in the garlic and sauté for 30 seconds. Add the tomatoes with their juice, fish stock, wine, and thyme. Raise the heat to medium-high and bring to a boil. Reduce the heat to medium-low, cover partially, and simmer for 1 minute to blend the flavors. Season to taste with salt and pepper.

2 Cook the seafood
Add the fish and mussels to the pan, discarding any mussels that do not close to the touch. Cover and simmer until the mussels open and the fish is just opaque throughout, 3–4 minutes. Add the crabmeat and simmer for 1 minute to heat through. Ladle into shallow bowls, discarding any mussels that failed to open, and serve.

cook's tip

Good fish stock is increasingly available at seafood and other specialty markets. Buy it in small containers and store in the freezer for up to 3 months.

cook's tip

Grilled or broiled broccoli florets,
are an easy accompaniment to
this dish. Toss the florets with
a drizzle of olive oil, sprinkle with
salt and pepper, then place in a
grill basket on the grill rack, or on
a baking sheet if broiling. Cook,
turning once or twice, until
tender-crisp and the edges are
charred, for 3–4 minutes.

herbed pork chops with apples

1 Season the pork chops

In a small bowl, stir together the sage, thyme, oregano, rosemary, ½ teaspoon salt, and ¼ teaspoon pepper. Season the pork chops on both sides with the herb mixture, patting it firmly into the meat. Place the chops on a large platter in a single layer and let stand for 10 minutes at room temperature, or cover and refrigerate for up to overnight.

2 Cook the pork

Meanwhile, prepare a gas or charcoal grill for direct-heat grilling over medium-high heat and oil the grill rack. Or, preheat a broiler (grill). When ready to cook, place the chops on the grill rack, or put on a rimmed baking sheet and place under the broiler. Cook, turning once or twice, until browned on the outside and barely pink inside, 8–12 minutes total.

3 Cook the apples

When the chops are about half done, brush the apples slices with the oil and place them around the pork at the edges of the grill rack where the heat is less intense, or around the chops on the baking sheet. Cook, turning once or twice, until lightly browned and tender, 4–6 minutes total. Cut the apple slices in half, and serve along with the chops.

Dried sage, 1 teaspoon

Dried thyme, 1 teaspoon

Dried oregano, 1 teaspoon

Dried rosemary, ¾ teaspoon

Salt and freshly ground pepper

Bone-in center-cut pork loin chops, 4, each about 1 inch (2.5 cm) thick

Tart apples such as Granny Smith, 2, cored and cut crosswise into slices ½ inch (12 mm) thick

Canola oil, 1 tablespoon

SERVES 4

fennel-crusted
pork tenderloin

Lemon, 1 large

Fennel seeds,
1 ½ tablespoons

Salt, 1 teaspoon

Black peppercorns,
2 ½ teaspoons coarsely
crushed

Garlic, 3 large cloves, finely
chopped

Olive oil, 1 ½ tablespoons

Pork tenderloin,
1 (about 1 ¼ lb/625 g) or
2 (about ¾ lb/375 g each)

SERVES 4–6

1 Prepare the pork

Grate 1 ½ teaspoons zest from the lemon and squeeze
1 tablespoon juice into a small bowl. Add the fennel seeds,
salt, pepper, garlic, and oil and stir to combine. Place the pork
in a roasting pan and rub all over with the spice mixture. Let
stand at room temperature for 5 minutes, or cover and
refrigerate for up to overnight.

2 Roast the pork

Preheat the oven to 425°F (220°C). Roast the pork
until it is browned on the outside and barely pink in the center
and an instant-read thermometer inserted into the center reads
145°–150°F (63°–65°C), about 12–15 minutes total. Transfer
the pork to a carving board, tent with aluminum foil, and let
stand for 10 minutes. Cut on the diagonal into slices ½ inch
(12 mm) thick, divide among 4 plates, and serve.

cook's tip

Roast chunks of potatoes, root
vegetables, or winter squash—
tossed with olive oil, salt, and
pepper—alongside the pork. Put
in the oven about 10 minutes
before roasting the pork. Stir the
vegetables often, and roast
until tender.

make more
to store

classic
roast chicken

ROAST CHICKEN

Whole chickens, 2, each about 3½ lb (1.75 kg)

Fresh rosemary or tarragon, 4 tablespoons (⅓ oz/10 g) minced

Salt and freshly ground pepper

Chicken broth, ¾ cup (6 fl oz/180 ml)

Dry white wine or chicken broth, ¼ cup (2 fl oz/60 ml)

SERVES 4

makes about 8 cups (3 lb/ 1.5 kg) cooked chicken total

Roast chicken is a wonderful supper centerpiece, but it's also great the next day. Here, you roast two birds, so that you have dinner tonight plus leftovers for making the recipes on the following pages.

1 Prepare the chickens
Preheat the oven to 450°F (230°C). Place the birds, breast side up, on a rack in a large roasting pan (or use 2 pans). Pat the chickens dry with paper towels. Rub the outside of each chicken with 2 tablespoons rosemary and a generous amount of salt and pepper.

2 Roast the chickens
Roast the chickens for 20 minutes. Reduce the oven temperature to 400°F (200°C) and continue to roast until an instant-read thermometer inserted into a thigh away from the bone registers 170°F (77°C), about 40 minutes longer. Transfer 1 chicken to a carving board and let rest for 10 minutes. Set the second chicken aside to cool before shredding the meat and storing (see Storage Tip, right).

3 Make the pan sauce
Discard all but about 1 tablespoon fat from the roasting pan. Place over medium-high heat and add the broth and wine. Bring to a boil and stir, scraping up the browned bits on the pan bottom. Cook until slightly reduced, about 1 minute. Season to taste with salt and pepper. Carve one of the chickens into serving pieces and divide among 4 plates. Top with the sauce and serve.

storage tip

To store the second chicken for use in the following recipes, let it cool, then remove the meat from the bones, discarding the skin and carcass. If you have pieces left from the first chicken, remove the meat from them as well. Shred the meat and store in an airtight container or resealable plastic bag in the refrigerator for up to 3 days.

cook's tip

Quesadillas are ideal for using up leftovers. Experiment with different combinations, such as black beans, shredded cheese, and fresh herbs or sliced smoked sausage and roasted red bell peppers (capsicums).

chicken & spinach
quesadillas

1 Prepare the filling

In a large, heavy frying pan over medium heat, warm 1 tablespoon of the oil. Add the mushrooms and sauté until tender, about 3 minutes. Add the spinach and chicken and sauté just until the spinach is wilted, about 30 seconds. Transfer to a bowl.

2 Assemble the quesadillas

Divide the chicken mixture among the tortillas, spooning it onto half of each tortilla and leaving a ¾-inch (2-cm) border uncovered. Sprinkle evenly with the cheese. Fold the tortillas in half over the chicken mixture to enclose loosely.

3 Cook the quesadillas

Wipe out the frying pan with a paper towel and return to medium heat. Brush lightly with the remaining oil. Working in batches, add the quesadillas to the pan and cook until golden brown on the first side, 1–2 minutes. Using a large spatula, carefully turn the quesadillas and cook until golden on the second side and the cheese is melted, 2–3 minutes longer. Divide the quesadillas among 4 plates and serve. Pass the sour cream and salsa at the table.

Roast Chicken, 2 cups (12 oz/375 g) shredded, homemade (page 76) or purchased

Corn oil, 3 tablespoons

Fresh button mushrooms, 6 oz (185 g), trimmed and sliced

Baby spinach, 2 cups (4 oz/125 g) packed

Flour tortillas, 8, each 10 inches (25 cm) in diameter

Monterey jack cheese, 2 cups (8 oz/250 g) shredded

Sour cream, ½ cup (4 oz/ 125 g)

Salsa, ½ cup (4 oz/125 g), homemade or purchased

SERVES 4

79

chicken couscous
with dried fruit

Roast Chicken, 2 cups (12 oz/375 g) shredded, homemade (page 76) or purchased

Lemons, 2

Olive oil, 4 tablespoons (2 fl oz/60 ml)

Yellow onion, 1 small, chopped

Garlic, 3 cloves, minced

Ground cumin, 1½ teaspoons

Ground cinnamon, ¾ teaspoon

Mixed dried fruits such as pitted dates and apricots, 1 cup (6 oz/185 g) chopped

Chicken broth, 3 cups (24 fl oz/750 ml)

Couscous, 2 cups (6 oz/185 g)

Fresh cilantro (fresh coriander), ¼ cup (⅓ oz/10 g) minced

Sliced (flaked) almonds, ½ cup (2 oz/60 g), toasted

SERVES 4

1 Cook the vegetables

Grate 1½ teaspoons zest from the lemons and squeeze ¼ cup (2 fl oz/60 ml) juice. In a large saucepan over medium heat, warm 3 tablespoons of the oil. Add the onion and sauté until softened, about 4 minutes. Add the garlic and sauté until the garlic and onion are golden, 1–2 minutes. Stir in the cumin and cinnamon, and then mix in the chicken, lemon zest and juice, dried fruits, and broth. Bring the mixture to a boil, reduce the heat to medium-low, cover, and simmer for 5 minutes to blend the flavors.

2 Cook the couscous

Stir in the couscous, re-cover the pan, and remove from the heat. Let stand until the liquid is absorbed and the couscous is softened, about 5 minutes. Add the cilantro and toss with a fork to fluff the couscous and distribute the cilantro. Garnish with the almonds and serve.

cook's tip

This one-dish meal is perfect for a picnic or potluck for two reasons: it is easily transported and it tastes great at room temperature. Make sure to refrigerate until about 1 hour before serving.

cook's tip

To prepare a mango, first peel it using a vegetable peeler or paring knife. Then, stand the mango on one of its narrow edges and use a sharp knife to cut down along one side of the stem end, just grazing the pit. Repeat on the other side. Cut each half into slices. Slice off any flesh left clinging to the pit.

chicken & mango salad

1 Make the vinaigrette
In a food processor or blender, combine the peanut oil, vinegar, mustard, and chile oil (if using) and process until blended. Add the garlic and chutney and continue to process to a smooth purée.

2 Assemble the salad
In a bowl, combine the chicken, celery, onion, cashews, and mango. Add the vinaigrette and toss gently to coat. Divide the lettuce among individual plates, top with the chicken mixture, and serve.

Roast Chicken, 2 cups (12 oz/375 g) shredded, homemade (page 76) or purchased

Peanut or canola oil, ⅔ cup (5 fl oz/160 ml)

White wine vinegar, ¼ cup (2 fl oz/60 ml)

Dijon mustard, 1 tablespoon

Asian chile oil, 2–3 teaspoons (optional)

Garlic, 2 cloves, minced

Mango chutney, ½ cup (5 oz/155 g)

Celery, 1 stalk, thinly sliced

Red onion, 1 small, halved and thinly sliced

Roasted salted cashews, ⅓ cup (2½ oz/75 g), coarsely chopped

Mango, 1, peeled, pitted, and thinly sliced

Romaine (cos) lettuce, 4 cups (4 oz/125 g) shredded

SERVES 4

chicken salad
provençal

Roast Chicken, 2 cups (12 oz/375 g) shredded or sliced, homemade (page 76) or purchased

Red wine vinegar, 3 tablespoons

Dijon mustard, 1 tablespoon

Olive oil, ⅓ cup (3 fl oz/ 80 ml)

Salt and freshly ground pepper

Red potatoes, 1 lb (500 g), small

Slender green beans, ½ lb (250 g), trimmed

Butter (Boston) lettuce, 1 small head, leaves separated

Plum (Roma) tomatoes, 3, cut into wedges

Niçoise olives, ½ cup (2½ oz/75 g)

Red onion, 1 small, thinly sliced

Fresh basil, ¼ cup (⅓ oz/10 g) slivered

SERVES 4

1 Make the vinaigrette
In a small bowl, whisk together the vinegar and mustard. Whisk in the oil. Season to taste with salt and pepper. Set aside.

2 Cook the vegetables
In a large saucepan, combine the potatoes with water to cover and a generous pinch of salt. Bring to a boil over high heat, reduce the heat to medium, and cook for 8 minutes. Add the green beans and continue to cook until the potatoes are tender when pierced with the tip of a knife and the green beans are crisp-tender, 2–3 minutes longer. Drain the potatoes and green beans. Let cool slightly. Slice the potatoes and place in a bowl. Add the beans and 3 tablespoons of the vinaigrette and toss to coat.

3 Assemble the salad
Line a platter or individual plates with the lettuce leaves. Arrange the chicken, potatoes, green beans, tomatoes, and olives on the lettuce. Sprinkle with the onion slices and basil. Drizzle with the remaining vinaigrette and serve.

cook's tip

The potatoes and green beans
can be cooked and the vinaigrette
prepared up to 1 day in advance.
Store them in airtight containers
in the refrigerator. Allow them
to come to room temperature
before serving.

braised
brisket

BRAISED BRISKET

Beef brisket, about 5 lb
(2.5 kg), trimmed of excess fat

Paprika, 1 tablespoon

**Salt and freshly ground
pepper**

Olive oil, 2 tablespoons

Yellow onions, 2, chopped

Celery, 3 stalks, chopped

Carrots, 2, chopped

Beef broth, 2 cups
(16 fl oz/500 ml)

Dry red wine, ¾ cup
(6 fl oz/180 ml)

Diced tomatoes, 1 can
(14½ oz/455 g), with juice

Fresh marjoram,
2 tablespoons minced

SERVES 4

makes about 10 cups
(4 lb/2 kg) sliced or
shredded brisket total

Flavorful brisket is an ideal candidate for oven braising. Serve it with its sauce the first night, and then use the rest of it for making the sandwiches, pasta, or savory pie on the following pages.

1 **Brown the meat**
Preheat the oven to 325°F (165°C). Season the brisket with the paprika and salt and pepper. In a large heavy pot or Dutch oven over medium-high heat, warm the oil. Add the brisket and cook, turning as needed, until well browned on all sides, about 10 minutes. Transfer to a platter.

2 **Cook the vegetables and the brisket**
Add the onions, celery, and carrots to the drippings in the pot and sauté over medium heat until the vegetables are softened, about 5 minutes. Pour in the broth and stir, scraping up the browned bits on the pot bottom. Stir in the wine and the tomatoes and their juice. Return the meat and any juices from the platter to the pot. Cover, transfer to the oven, and cook until the brisket is fork-tender, 3–3½ hours.

3 **Make the sauce**
Transfer the brisket to a carving board and let rest for 10 minutes. Spoon off and discard the fat from the liquid in the pot. Place the pot over medium-high heat and bring the liquid to a boil. Stir in the marjoram, reduce the heat to medium, and simmer until the liquid is reduced by one-fourth, 7–10 minutes. Taste the sauce and season with salt and pepper. Slice the brisket across the grain and serve with some of the sauce and vegetables spooned on top.

storage tip

To store the leftover brisket, place it, uncut or shredded, in an airtight container. Put the sauce in a separate airtight container. Refrigerate the meat and sauce for up to 3 days.

cook's tip

You will find many good-quality
commercial barbecue sauces
on the market today. If you would
rather have a less saucy sandwich,
instead of immersing the meat
in the sauce when warming it,
pour the sauce into a small bowl
and use a basting brush to smear
it on the meat.

bbq brisket
sandwiches

1 Warm the brisket
In a frying pan over medium heat, warm the barbecue sauce. Add the brisket slices or the shredded brisket and turn in the sauce until heated through.

2 Assemble the sandwiches
Lightly toast the rolls. Place the roll bottoms, cut side up, on individual plates and divide the brisket among them, moistening the meat on each sandwich with some of the sauce. Close the sandwiches with the tops and serve.

Braised Brisket, 2 cups (12 oz/375 g) sliced or shredded (page 86)

Barbecue sauce, 1/2 cup (4 fl oz/120 ml)

Crusty sandwich rolls, 4, sliced in half

SERVES 4

pappardelle
with beef ragù

Braised Brisket, 2 cups
(12 oz/375 g) shredded
(page 86)

Sauce from brisket, 1 cup
(8 fl oz/250 ml)

Pancetta or bacon, 2 oz
(60 g), diced

Leeks, 2 large, white and pale
green parts, halved, washed,
and thinly sliced

Fennel bulb, 1 small,
trimmed and chopped

Garlic, 2 cloves, minced

Diced tomatoes, 1 can
(14½ oz/455 g), with juice

Fresh basil, ¼ cup
(⅓ oz/10 g) minced

Salt

**Pappardelle or other wide
egg noodles,** ¾ lb (375 g)

Parmesan cheese, ½ cup
(2 oz/60 g) freshly grated

SERVES 4

1 **Cook the vegetables**
In a large frying pan over medium heat, cook the
pancetta, stirring occasionally, until browned, about 5 minutes.
Using a slotted spoon, transfer the pancetta to a small plate.
Add the leeks and fennel to the drippings in the pan and sauté
until softened, about 5 minutes. Add the garlic and sauté until
softened, about 1 minute.

2 **Make the ragù**
Add the brisket, sauce, and tomatoes and their juice
to the pan. Raise the heat to high and bring to a gentle boil.
Reduce the heat to medium and simmer, stirring occasionally,
until the flavors are blended and the sauce is slightly reduced,
about 10 minutes. Stir in the basil and cook for 1 minute
longer. Stir in the reserved pancetta.

3 **Cook the pasta**
While the ragù is simmering, bring a large pot of water
to a boil. Add 2 tablespoons salt and the pasta and cook,
stirring occasionally to prevent sticking, until the pasta is al dente,
according to the package directions. Drain the pasta, add
it to the sauce, and toss to coat. Divide among shallow bowls
and serve. Pass the cheese at the table.

cook's tip

This rich, meaty ragù is excellent tossed with fettucine, linguine, or bucatini. It can also be added to ¾ lb (375 g) cooked penne, ziti, or gemelli piled into a baking dish, and topped with shredded mozzerella cheese. Bake at 375°F (190°C) until warmed through, about 10 minutes.

cook's tip

The mashed potatoes can be
prepared up to 2 days in advance.
Store them in an airtight container
in the refrigerator. This is also an
excellent way to use up leftover
mashed potatoes. Make sure you
have 3 cups (24 oz/750 g) total.

shepherd's
pie

1 Cook the potatoes

In a large saucepan, combine the potatoes, water to cover, and a generous pinch of salt. Bring to a boil over high heat, reduce the heat to medium, and cook until tender when pierced with the tip of a knife, 12–15 minutes. Drain well. Pass the potatoes through a ricer into a bowl, or mash in the bowl with a potato masher. Add the milk and 1 tablespoon of the butter and beat with a wooden spoon or with a handheld mixer on medium speed until smooth and fluffy. Season with ½ teaspoon salt and ¼ teaspoon pepper.

2 Simmer the filling

While the potatoes are cooking, in another large saucepan over medium heat, melt the remaining 1 tablespoon butter. Add the onion and carrots and cook, stirring often, until softened, about 5 minutes. Stir in the peas, brisket, sauce, and thyme. Bring to a simmer and cook, stirring occasionally, until heated through, 7–10 minutes.

3 Assemble and cook

Preheat the broiler (grill). Spoon the hot filling into a shallow 9-inch (23-cm) square baking dish. Spread the potatoes evenly over the filling. Place under the broiler and broil (grill) until the potatoes are tinged with brown, about 1 minute. Serve directly from the baking dish.

Braised Brisket, 3 cups (18 oz/560 g) shredded, (page 86)

Sauce from brisket, 2 cups (16 fl oz/500 ml), or 1 cup (8 fl oz/250 ml) beef broth

Russet potatoes, 2 lb (1 kg), peeled and cut into chunks

Salt and freshly ground pepper

Milk or half-and-half (half cream), ¾ cup (6 fl oz/ 180 ml)

Unsalted butter, 2 tablespoons

Yellow onion, 1 small, finely chopped

Carrots, 2, finely chopped

Frozen baby peas, ¾ cup (4 oz/125 g), thawed

Fresh thyme, 1 tablespoon chopped

SERVES 4

93

the smarter cook

The secret to getting dinner on the table during a hectic workweek isn't spending more time in the kitchen, it's cooking smarter. And you can do just that with inspired recipes, a well-stocked pantry, a weekly meal plan, and a few strategic shopping trips. Your efforts will yield simple, satisfying dishes in less than 30 minutes, giving you more time to sit down to a home-cooked supper with your family.

Keep your pantry well stocked, and you have the foundation for all your weekday suppers. Plan your menus, and you'll make fewer trips to the store. Cook an extra roast chicken or slow-braised brisket on the weekend, and you can use it in other recipes later in the week. In the following pages, you'll find tips on how to manage your time and stock your kitchen—the keys to becoming a smarter cook.

get started

The keys to cooking delicious dinners every night of the week are planning and organization. This means keeping a well-stocked pantry (page 104), putting together a weekly meal plan, and giving careful thought to how preparing dinner fits into your schedule. With these simple strategies in place, you'll save hours of kitchen and shopping time and have more time for you and your family.

plan a weeknight meal

▥ **Look at the whole week.** During the weekend, take time to think about how many meals you'll need to prepare in the week ahead. A good strategy is to plan at least one menu with a main dish that can be doubled with little extra effort, like the hearty brisket recipe in chapter 3, so you can use the leftovers as the base of a meal later in the week. Then choose additional recipes to round out the week. You'll want to keep your menus varied—pasta or soup and salad one night, an Asian main dish with rice or an Italian vegetable stew over polenta the next.

▥ **Let the seasons be your guide.** Choose main dishes that match the weather: hearty, sustaining stews and roasts in winter, light pastas and salads as the weather warms up. This will allow you to take full advantage of each season's best fresh ingredients. You'll probably save money, too, because in-season foods are often less expensive.

▥ **Match your menus to your schedule.** Once you've picked your main dishes, you can decide which night will work best for each. For the busiest days, choose recipes that can be made mostly or entirely ahead of time.

▥ **Get everyone involved.** Enlist kids and other family members to help plan the week's menus and they'll enjoy each meal more. Encourage them to help you with the preparation, too.

▥ **Cook on the weekend.** If possible, prepare some or all of Monday night's meal over the weekend. You can also cook a double batch of a dish that freezes well, such as a stew, curry, or soup, and store half of it in the freezer for future use (see page 106 for freezing tips).

THINK SEASONALLY

Here is a guide to using the best that each season has to offer whenever you are making the recipes in this book.

spring Serve light main dishes, salads, soups, and pastas that call for asparagus, fennel, fresh herbs (such as dill, chives, parsley, and mint), green (spring) onions, new potatoes, peas, and lamb.

summer Serve grilled meat, seafood, or poultry along with pastas, soups, and salads that feature arugula (rocket), avocados, bell peppers (capsicums), corn, cucumbers, green beans, fresh herbs (such as basil, thyme, and parsley), tomatoes, and zucchini (courgettes).

autumn Serve sustaining soups, pastas, and roasted meats made with slow-simmered vegetables, including butternut or acorn squash, cauliflower, fresh herbs (such as sage, bay leaves, and rosemary), leeks, mushrooms, potatoes, and yams.

winter Serve hearty stews, braised dishes, and soups that include beets, cabbage, fresh herbs (such as rosemary and sage), hearty greens like kale and Swiss chard, mushrooms, parsnips, rutabagas, turnips, and winter squashes.

round it out

Once you have decided what dish to make as the centerpiece of your meal, choose among a wide variety of appealing side dishes to round out the menu. Keep in mind both speed and ease of preparation.

salad To save time, buy packaged, prewashed greens. Choose salad ingredients that complement the main dish: a salad with lettuce, cucumbers, and an Asian-style dressing to accompany a Thai curry, or an arugula, tomato, and shaved Parmesan salad dressed with olive oil and lemon juice to serve with an Italian pasta. Make extra dressing and store it in the refrigerator for use throughout the week.

fresh vegetables You can steam, blanch, or roast many vegetables ahead of time, refrigerate them, and reheat them at dinnertime. Or, serve the vegetables at room temperature, drizzled with a vinaigrette or with olive oil and lemon juice.

roasted vegetables In the time it takes to put together the main dish, you can also roast vegetables. Start with precut fresh produce, such as broccoli and cauliflower florets, butternut squash, or asparagus spears. Toss the vegetables in a little olive oil and roast in a single layer on a baking sheet at 425°F (220°C) for 10–20 minutes (depending on the vegetable), stirring occasionally. Season with salt and pepper and serve.

braised greens Buy packaged, prewashed greens, such as spinach or mixed braising greens, and cook them in olive oil. For sturdier greens such as kale, add a small amount of broth and cook, covered, until tender.

potatoes Buy small new potatoes, coat them with olive oil, and sprinkle with salt before roasting as you would other vegetables (see above). Or, boil larger potatoes in salted water for 20–30 minutes, let them cool, and keep them in the refrigerator for later use.

rice Cook white or brown rice ahead of time and refrigerate or freeze in resealable plastic bags.

couscous Instant couscous, available plain or in a variety of seasoned blends, takes less than 10 minutes to prepare on the stovetop.

polenta Quick-cooking polenta is also ready to serve in less than 10 minutes. Make a double batch, add some Parmesan cheese, and serve half. Pour the rest into a baking pan, cover with plastic wrap, and refrigerate for another meal. When you're ready to use the polenta, cut it into squares or triangles and fry in olive oil in a nonstick pan until browned on both sides.

artisanal bread Warm crusty bread briefly in the oven, slice it, and serve with butter or good-quality olive oil.

tomatoes Slice fresh, ripe tomatoes, arrange the slices on a platter, and season them with olive oil, salt, and freshly ground pepper. If desired, sprinkle with crumbled feta cheese, olives, or chopped fresh herbs.

cucumbers Toss sliced cucumbers with vinaigrette and chopped fresh herbs as an accompaniment to fish. Or, dress the slices with rice vinegar, Asian sesame oil, a pinch of sugar, and a sprinkling of toasted sesame seeds to serve alongside Asian dishes.

easy desserts For nights when you have time to prepare dessert, try these quick ideas: seasonal fresh fruit drizzled with honey, cream, or yogurt; ice cream topped with nuts and warm chocolate sauce, caramel sauce, or hot coffee; a selection of cheeses, served with sliced apples, dried fruit, and walnuts.

sample meals

These weekly meals give you ideas for a more leisurely Sunday night supper, followed by suggestions for quick dinners on busy weeknights. When you cook a chicken or brisket at the beginning of the week, you'll have leftovers to use for a quickly assembled second main dish a few days later, giving you a head start on that second night.

SAMPLE WEEK 1	SAMPLE WEEK 2	SAMPLE WEEK 3
SUNDAY	**SUNDAY**	**SUNDAY**
Classic Roast Chicken (page 76)	**Braised Brisket** (page 86)	**Classic Roast Chicken** (page 76)
Rice pilaf Sautéed zucchini with oregano	Mashed potatoes Braised winter greens	Roasted butternut squash Sautéed green beans with butter
MONDAY	**MONDAY**	**MONDAY**
Farfalle with Salsa Cruda (page 36)	**Spring Vegetable Risotto** (page 64)	**Chicken Salad Provençal** (page 84)
Mixed salad greens with vinaigrette	Red leaf lettuce with blue cheese dressing	Garlic crostini
TUESDAY	**TUESDAY**	**TUESDAY**
Fennel-Crusted Pork Tenderloin (page 72)	**Pappardelle with Beef Ragù** (page 90)	**Sausages with White Beans** (page 18)
Roasted acorn squash	Shaved zucchini & Parmesan	Warm focaccia wedges
WEDNESDAY	**WEDNESDAY**	**WEDNESDAY**
Chicken Couscous with Dried Fruit (page 80)	**Lemongrass Chicken & Asparagus** (page 26)	**Herbed Spinach Frittata with Feta** (page 59)
Spinach salad with feta & almonds	Steamed white rice	Mixed salad greens with vinaigrette
THURSDAY	**THURSDAY**	**THURSDAY**
Miso-Glazed Salmon with Bok Choy (page 17)	**Polenta with Vegetable Ragout** (page 48)	**Balsamic Chicken & Peppers** (page 60)
Steamed white rice	Pan-fried Italian sausages	Roasted potato wedges
FRIDAY	**FRIDAY**	**FRIDAY**
Steaks with Herb Butter (page 10)	**Moroccan Lamb Burgers** (page 52)	**Herbed Pork Chops with Apples** (page 71)
Sliced tomatoes with olive oil	Mixed salad greens with vinaigrette	Steamed broccoli florets Baked yams

Prep ahead. Use a food processor to make quick work of chopping vegetables. Double up vegetable prep by chopping extra vegetables for 1 or 2 other recipes one night and then storing them in an airtight container in the refrigerator for use the next night.

Get the right tools. You don't need a lot of fancy equipment to prepare a good dinner. Make sure you have these basic tools and your cooking will be faster, easier, and more enjoyable: an 8-inch (20-cm) chef's knife, a paring knife, a steel or other knife sharpener, a few heavy-bottomed saucepans and nonstick frying pans, wooden spoons, and heat-resistant silicone spatulas. Keep the tools you use most within easy reach.

Use the grill. A gas grill or broiler (grill) can help you create flavorful main dishes in minutes. Grill vegetables alongside the main dish as an accompaniment, or take advantage of the hot grill after the meal is served to grill vegetables for use the following night. Marinate meats and vegetables ahead of time for great flavor combinations.

Clean as you go. Before you begin cooking, empty the dishwasher. Wash pots, pans, and utensils as you cook, so that when you sit down to eat, the kitchen work surfaces are clear. This will save cleanup time after dinner.

Get help. Ask family members to assist in setting the table, assembling and cutting up the ingredients, and doing the dishes afterward.

shortcut suppers

Some days you just don't have the time to plan meals or to shop. For those occasions, here are ideas for dinners that can be put together very quickly.

Rotisserie chicken Buy a chicken that is large enough for dinner plus leftovers. Cut up the leftover meat to make any of the recipes that follow Classic Roast Chicken (page 76).

Cooked sausages Keep fully cooked meat- or poultry-based sausages, such as Italian, chicken-apple, and kielbasa, in the refrigerator or freezer. Panfry the sausages along with apple slices until browned.

Egg dishes Make sure there is a supply of eggs in the refrigerator for making a frittata (page 59) or an omelet using chopped vegetables, cheese, and leftover chicken, ham, or sausages.

Quesadillas Keep flour tortillas in the refrigerator for preparing quesadillas (page 79) or tacos using cheese and leftover chicken, sausage slices, or vegetables. Stock up on salsa, rice, and canned refried, pinto, or black beans to round out the menu.

Pasta Have spaghetti and linguine on hand, along with prepared pasta sauces. To make a quick sauce, cook chopped garlic and red pepper flakes in olive oil, then toss with cooked spaghetti and garnish with chopped parsley and grated Parmesan cheese.

Pizza Keep a prebaked pizza crust in the refrigerator. Top with leftover meat, vegetables, and grated cheese. Bake in a 450°F (230°C) oven until the crust is heated through and the cheese is melted.

Main-dish salads Always have packaged, prewashed lettuce, mixed salad greens, or baby spinach in the crisper of your refrigerator. Toss with salad dressing and top with slices of leftover steak, chicken, or fish, canned tuna, or hard-boiled eggs, olives, and tomatoes.

Open-faced sandwiches Pile leftover meat or vegetables on slices of crusty bread to make open-faced sandwiches. Top with slices of fresh mozzarella or provolone and broil (grill) until the cheese melts.

shop smarter

Using the freshest produce and other high-quality ingredients will help ensure great-tasting dinners and healthier eating. Seek out a butcher, fishmonger, produce store, and specialty-food shop that stock top-notch ingredients at reasonable prices and patronize them regularly. Arrange to call ahead and place your order, so it's ready to pick up on your way home from work.

▥ **Produce** When at the market, ask which fruits and vegetables are at their peak of flavor and ripeness. If there is a regular farmers' market in your area, get in the habit of visiting it once a week. It's an excellent way to stay in touch with what is in season, and you'll often find good deals on bumper-crop produce. Choose vegetables and fruits that are free of bruises and blemishes and feel heavy for their size. Greens and herbs should be crisp and brightly colored, and vegetables such as eggplants (aubergines) and zucchini (courgettes) should have taut skins and be firm to the touch.

▥ **Meat & poultry** Look for meat with good, uniform color and a fresh smell. Any fat should be bright white rather than grayish. Poultry should be plump, with smooth skin and firm flesh, and any visible fat should be white to light yellow. If you need boned meat or poultry, ask the butcher to do it for you, to save you time in the kitchen.

▥ **Seafood** Look for fish and shellfish with bright color, a moist surface, and little or no "fishy" smell. Ask the purveyor which fish and shellfish are freshest. If possible, use seafood the same day you purchase it.

▥ **Broth & stock** Good-quality broths can be found in cans and aseptic boxes on market shelves. Read the labels carefully to avoid unwholesome ingredients and, if possible, purchase organic brands for both better health and flavor. Many specialty-food shops sell their own made-from-scratch fresh or frozen broths, which are another good option.

▥ **Wine** Ask your wine merchant to recommend good everyday red and white wines at reasonable prices. Buy wine by the case, so you always have a supply on hand; you often will get a discount for buying in bulk.

MAKE A SHOPPING LIST

prepare in advance Make a list of what you need to buy before you go shopping and you'll save time at the store.

make a template Create a list template on your computer, then fill it in during the week before you go shopping.

categorize your lists Use the following categories to keep your lists organized: pantry, fresh, and occasional.

▥ **pantry items** Check the pantry and write down any items that need to be restocked to make the meals on your weekly plan.

▥ **fresh ingredients** These are for immediate use and include produce, seafood, meats, and some cheeses. You might need to visit different stores or supermarket sections, so divide the list into subcategories, such as produce, dairy, and meats.

▥ **occasional items** This is a revolving list for refrigerated items that are replaced as needed, such as butter and eggs.

be flexible Be ready to change your menus based on the freshest ingredients at the market.

PANTRY ITEMS

balsamic vinegar

black pepper

canned whole plum (Roma) tomatoes

chicken broth

dry white wine

garlic

olive oil

red pepper flakes

salt

white rice

FRESH: PRODUCE

asparagus

baby spinach

basil

bok choy

lemons

FRESH: CHEESE

feta

mozzarella

FRESH: MEATS & SEAFOOD

bacon

hot Italian sausages

salmon fillets

skinless, boneless chicken breasts

turkey cutlets

OCCASIONAL ITEMS

eggs

Parmesan cheese

unsalted butter

make the most of your time

Once you've planned your meals for the week, give some thought to how you will organize your time. The more you can do in advance, the more quickly and easily a meal will come together when you are ready to prepare and serve it.

▪ **Stock up.** Over the weekend, check the pantry or refrigerator for the staples you'll need during the week. Also check your supply of basic nonperishable ingredients, so you can improvise a quick meal or side dish. See pages 98–99 for suggestions.

▪ **Shop less.** If you've made a weekly meal plan, you should need to shop only two or three times a week for fresh ingredients, such as produce, meat, poultry, or seafood.

▪ **Do it ahead.** Do as much as you can ahead of time. For example, chop or slice vegetables or simply gather ingredients in the morning to save time in the evening. Some dishes rely on specific do-ahead steps, such as marinating, which is described in the recipe. Remember, too, many stews, soups, and pasta sauces can be made a day or two ahead and refrigerated (or frozen for a longer period), leaving you with only a little work to do just before dinner.

▪ **Double up.** When making a soup, stew, or roast chicken, make enough to use for more than one meal. For example, prepare two chickens and serve one with rice and a vegetable one night. Later in the week, make a main-course salad. Then, use the rest in a couscous dish.

▪ **Cook smarter.** Before you begin, reread the recipe carefully. As you review it, take note of any time-saving steps, such as simultaneously mixing the eggs for a frittata while the vegetable filling cooks (page 59), or seasoning and cooking shrimp while the accompanying rice steams (page 56). Then, do as professional chefs do and assemble, prep, and measure all the fresh and pantry ingredients you'll need to make the dish. Get out all the equipment required at the same time, so everything is ready to go. Finally, set out the serving dishes. Now, you are ready to begin cooking.

the well-stocked kitchen

Smart cooking is all about being prepared. If your pantry, refrigerator, and freezer are well stocked and organized, you'll always have a good head start on making supper. And if you keep track of what is in your kitchen, you'll shop less often and you'll spend less time in the store when you do.

On the pages that follow, you'll find a guide to all the ingredients you'll need to have on hand to make the recipes in this book, plus dozens of tips for keeping them fresh and properly stored. Use the lists to find out what you already have in your kitchen and what you need to buy when you go shopping. The time you spend shopping and putting your kitchen in order will be time well spent—an investment in smarter cooking that pays off whenever you need to put dinner on the table.

the pantry

The pantry is typically a closet or one or more cupboards in which you store dried herbs and spices, pasta and grains, canned goods, and such fresh ingredients as garlic, onions, shallots, and any root vegetables that don't require refrigeration. Make sure that it is relatively cool, dry, dark when not in use, and away from the heat of the stove, which can hasten spoilage.

stock your pantry

- Take inventory of what is in your pantry using the Pantry Staples list.

- Remove everything from the pantry; clean the shelves and reline with paper, if needed; and then resort the items by type.

- Discard items that have passed their expiration date or have a stale or otherwise questionable appearance.

- Make a list of items that you need to replace or stock.

- Shop for the items on your list.

- Restock the pantry, organizing items by type so everything is easy to find.

- Write the purchase date on perishable items and clearly label bulk items.

- Keep staples you use often toward the front of the pantry.

- Keep dried herbs and spices in separate containers and preferably in a separate spice or herb organizer, shelf, or drawer.

keep it organized

- Look over the recipes in your weekly meal plan and check your pantry to make sure you have all the ingredients you'll need.

- Rotate items as you use them, moving the oldest ones to the front of the pantry so they will be used first.

- Keep a list of the items you use up so that you can replace them.

PANTRY STORAGE

dried herbs & spices Dried herbs and spices start losing flavor after 6 months, so buy them in small quantities and replace often. Store in airtight containers.

oils Store unopened bottles of oil at room temperature in a cool, dark place. Oils will keep for up to 1 year, but their flavor diminishes over time. Store opened bottles for 3 months at room temperature or in the refrigerator for up to 6 months.

grains & pasta Store grains in airtight containers for up to 3 months. The shelf life of most dried pastas is 1 year. Although safe to eat beyond that time, they will have lost flavor. Once you open a package, put what you don't cook into an airtight container.

fresh foods Store in a cool, dark place and check occasionally for sprouting or spoilage. Don't put potatoes alongside onions; when placed next to each other, they produce gases that hasten spoilage.

canned foods Discard canned foods if the can shows signs of expansion or buckling. Once a can is opened, transfer the unused contents to an airtight container and refrigerate.

DRIED HERBS & SPICES

bay leaves

black peppercorns

cayenne pepper

chili powder

Chinese five-spice powder

dried oregano

dried rosemary

dried sage

dried thyme

fennel seeds

ground allspice

ground cinnamon

ground cumin

mustard seeds

paprika

red pepper flakes

salt

OILS

Asian chile oil

Asian sesame oil

canola oil

corn oil

olive oil

peanut oil

VINEGARS

balsamic vinegar

red wine vinegar

rice vinegar

sherry vinegar

white wine vinegar

CANNED & JARRED FOODS

anchovies

apple cider

Asian fish sauce

beef broth

chicken broth

chunky peanut butter

coconut milk

curry paste, Thai red

diced tomatoes

Dijon mustard

honey Dijon mustard

mango chutney

Niçoise olives

roasted red bell peppers (capsicums)

salsa

sauerkraut

soy sauce

tomato paste

vegetable broth

white beans, such as cannellini

PASTAS & GRAINS

Arborio rice

Chinese egg noodles

couscous

farfalle pasta

long-grain white rice

orzo pasta

pappardelle pasta

penne pasta

polenta, quick-cooking

WINES & SPIRITS

dry red wine

dry sherry

dry white wine

Madeira

mirin

sake

MISCELLANEOUS

dark brown sugar

dried fruits: pitted dates and apricots

flour

flour tortillas

granulated sugar

peanuts

pita bread

raisins

roasted cashews

FRESH FOODS

apples

garlic

ginger

lemons

limes

oranges

red onions

red potatoes

russet potatoes

shallots

tomatoes

yellow onions

Yukon gold potatoes

the refrigerator & freezer

Once you have stocked and organized your pantry, you can apply the same time-saving principles to your refrigerator and freezer. Used for short-term cold storage, the refrigerator is ideal for storing your meats, poultry, vegetables, and leftovers. Done properly, freezing will preserve most of the flavor and nutrients in fruits and vegetables, and is an especially good way to store stocks, soups, and stews.

general tips

▦ Foods lose flavor under refrigeration, so proper storage and an even temperature of below 40°F (5°C) are important.

▦ Freeze foods at 0°F (-18°C) or below to retain color, texture, and flavor.

▦ Don't crowd foods in the refrigerator or freezer. Air should circulate freely to keep foods evenly cooled.

▦ To prevent freezer burn, use only moistureproof wrappings, such as aluminum foil, airtight plastic containers, or resealable plastic bags.

leftover storage

▦ You can store most prepared main dishes in an airtight container in the refrigerator for up to 4 days or in the freezer for up to 4 months.

▦ Check the contents of the refrigerator at least once a week and promptly discard old or spoiled food.

▦ Let food cool to room temperature before storing in the refrigerator or freezer. Transfer the cooled food to an airtight plastic or glass container, leaving room for expansion. Or put it in a resealable freezer bag, expelling as much air as possible before sealing.

▦ Freezing soups and stews in small batches allows you to heat up just enough to serve one or two people.

▦ Thaw frozen foods in the refrigerator or in the microwave. To avoid bacterial contamination, never thaw at room temperature.

KEEP IT ORGANIZED

clean first Remove items a few at a time and wash the refrigerator thoroughly with warm, soapy water, then rinse well with clear water. Wash and rinse your freezer at the same time.

rotate items Check the expiration dates on refrigerated items and discard any that have exceeded their time. Also, toss out any items that look questionable.

stock up Use the list on the opposite page as a starting point to decide what items you need to buy or replace.

shop Shop for the items on your list.

date of purchase Label items that you plan to keep for more than a few weeks, writing the date directly on the package or on a piece of masking tape.

WINE STORAGE

Once a wine bottle is uncorked, the wine is exposed to air, eventually causing it to taste like vinegar. Store opened wine in the refrigerator for up to 3 days. Use a vacuum wine pump to stopper the bottle.

fresh herb & vegetable storage

▥ Trim the stem ends of a bunch of parsley, stand the bunch in a glass of water, drape a plastic bag loosely over the leaves, and refrigerate. Wrap other fresh herbs in a damp paper towel, slip into a plastic bag, and store in the crisper. Rinse and stem all herbs just before using.

▥ Store tomatoes and eggplants (aubergines) at room temperature.

▥ Cut about ½ inch (12 mm) off the end of each asparagus spear; stand the spears, tips up, in a glass of cold water; and refrigerate, changing the water daily. The asparagus will keep for up to 1 week.

▥ Rinse leafy greens, such as chard, spin dry in a salad spinner, wrap in damp paper towels, and store in a resealable plastic bag in the crisper for up to 1 week. In general, store other vegetables in resealable bags in the crisper and rinse before using. Sturdy vegetables will keep for up to a week; more delicate ones will keep for only a few days.

meat, poultry & seafood storage

▥ Most seafood should be used the same day you purchase it. Place clams or mussels in a bowl, cover with a damp towel, and use within a day.

▥ Use fresh meat and poultry within 2 days of purchase. If buying packaged meats, check the expiration date and use before that date.

▥ Place packaged meats on a plate in the coldest part of the refrigerator. If only part of a package is used, discard the original wrapping and rewrap in fresh wrapping.

cheese storage

▥ Wrap all cheeses well to prevent them from drying out. Hard cheeses, such as Parmesan, have a low moisture content, so they keep longer than fresh cheeses, such as mozzarella. Use fresh cheeses within a couple days. Store soft and semisoft cheeses for up to 2 weeks and hard cheeses for up to 1 month.

index

weldonowen

415 Jackson Street, Suite 200, San Francisco, CA 94111
www.wopublishing.com

MEALS IN MINUTES SERIES

Conceived and produced by Weldon Owen Inc.

Copyright © 2006 by Weldon Owen Inc. and Williams-Sonoma, Inc.

The recipes in this book have been previously published as *Weeknight* in the Food Made Fast series.

All rights reserved, including the right of reproduction in whole or in part in any form.

Printed by 1010 Printing in China

Set in Formata
This edition first printed in 2012
10 9 8 7 6 5 4 3 2 1

Library of Congress Cataloging-in-Publication data is available.

Weldon Owen is a division of
BONNIER

Photographers Tucker + Hossler
Food Stylist Kevin Crafts
Food Stylist's Assistants Luis Bustamante, Alexa Hyman
Prop Stylist Leigh Nöe
Text Writer Steve Siegelman

ACKNOWLEDGMENTS
Weldon Owen wishes to thank the following people
for their generous support in producing this book:
Davina Baum, Heather Belt, Carrie Bradley, Ken DellaPenta,
Judith Dunham, Marianne Mitten, Sharon Silva, Robin Turk,
and Kate Washington.

Photographs by Bill Bettencourt: pages 8–9, 34–35, 38–39
(tip and recipe), 46–47 (recipe), 50–51 (recipe), 54–55 (recipe),
72–73 (recipe), 74–75, 76–77 (recipe), 86–87 (recipe).

ISBN-13: 978-1-61628-387-2
ISBN-10: 1-61628-387-4

A NOTE ON WEIGHTS AND MEASURES
All recipes include customary U.S. and metric measurements. Metric conversions are based on
a standard developed for these books and have been rounded off. Actual weights may vary.